SCOTTISH COUNTRY RECIPES

compiled by
Johanna Mathie

with illustrations of Scottish life by
H. J. Dobson RSW

Better wait on the cook
than on the doctor.
Scottish Proverb

SALMON

Index

Annie Hogg's Sweetbreads 32
Apple & Bramble Crumble 31
Ayrshire Bacon Dumplings 7
Baked Apples with
  Walnut Butterscotch Sauce 34
Boiled Cake 39
Bread Patties 27
Bruléed Raspberries with Whisky 46
Butterscotch Shortbread 45
Caramel Shortbread 19
Cheese Soup & Dumplings 21
Claggum 14
Fife Bannocks 37
Ginger Flapjacks 22
Granny McKie's Apple Chutney 8
Honey Cake 26
Honey Ice Cream 18
Honey Oat Breakfast 42

Mince & Tatties 24
Mustard Lamb and
  Turnip Purry 13
Oatmeal Sausages 3
Onion Gravy 38
Poacher's Soup 40
Porridge Oat Pastry 10
Rabbit Casserole 23
Rich Beef Stew 6
Rich Venison Casserole 47
Roastit Bubbly-jock 15
Roast Pheasant 35
Savoury Potato Cakes 16
Scots Tablet 30
Steak in Whisky Sauce 43
Stoved Bacon & Turnip 5
Stoved Chicken 29
Vegetable Broth 11

Cover *front:* Hearth and Home *by Erskine Nicol*
back: The Crofter's Cottage *by Richard Ansdell*
Title page: Granny's Blessing

Printed and Published by Dorrigo, Manchester, England. © Copyright.

Oatmeal Sausages

This recipe is ideal for using up left-over chicken.

1 oz butter	4 oz oatmeal
1 oz onion, finely chopped	Salt and pepper
2 rashers bacon, diced	A little left-over chicken, chopped finely
½ pt water	1 egg, beaten

3 oz dry white breadcrumbs

Melt the butter in a pan and fry the onion and bacon together until the onion is soft. Add the water and bring to the boil. Sprinkle in the oatmeal. Cover and cook for 15 to 20 minutes. Stir in seasoning to taste and the chopped chicken. Set aside to cool. When cold, roll into sausage shapes and dip in the beaten egg. Roll in the breadcrumbs and fry until golden brown, turning as necessary. Serves 2-4.

Highland Grace

Stoved Bacon and Turnip

In Scotland the word turnip is used to describe the vegetable which, elsewhere, is known as a swede. In fact, a swede is, properly, a 'Swedish turnip'.

1 large turnip (swede), peeled and cut into slices ¼ inch thick
8 rashers of smoked bacon   1 small onion, sliced thinly

Gently fry the bacon rashers in a large saucepan for two minutes (no oil may be needed if the bacon used produces enough fat). Set the rashers aside. Now build up alternate layers in the saucepan, starting with 2 rashers of bacon and a little onion, followed by a layer of turnip (swede) slices and so on. Add 2 tablespoons of cold water and simmer gently over a very low heat until cooked through. This dish makes a delicious accompaniment to roast chicken or game.

Rich Beef Stew

Delicious served with Ayrshire Bacon Dumplings.

1 lb stewing steak, cubed	¼ small turnip (swede), diced
A little oil for browning meat	¼ lb mushrooms, sliced
1 large onion, chopped roughly	2 tablespoons tomato purée
4 oz smoked bacon rashers, diced	1 teaspoon redcurrant jelly
2 tablespoons oatmeal	1 pt beef stock

5 fl oz red wine

First brown the steak on all sides in a little oil in a flameproof casserole, then add the onions and cook for 2 minutes. Add the bacon and cook for a further 2 minutes. Remove from the heat, stir in the oatmeal and then add the diced turnip (swede) and the mushrooms. Add the tomato purée and redcurrant jelly, pour in the stock and wine and stir well. Return to the heat, bring slowly to simmering point, cover and cook slowly for about 1½ to 2 hours until the meat is tender. Check seasoning before serving. Serves 4-6.

Ayrshire Bacon Dumplings

These dumplings make a tasty addition to casseroles, soups and stews.

6 oz self raising flour
Salt and pepper
$1/2$ teaspoon dried mixed herbs
3 oz shredded suet

2 teaspoons chopped fresh parsley or
1 teaspoon dried parsley
A little water to bind
3 oz smoked bacon rashers, finely chopped

In a bowl, mix together the flour and seasoning, add the mixed herbs and parsley and mix well. Rub in the suet, adding just enough water to make a firm dough. Shape into 12 balls. Make an indentation with the thumb in each ball and push in a little chopped bacon. Dampen the edges, pinch together and re-roll the ball. The finished dumplings can be boiled in a saucepan of water for about 40 to 50 minutes or can be added to casseroles or soups or stews for the equivalent time before the end of the cooking period.

Granny McKie's Apple Chutney

*This tangy chutney is easy to prepare and makes an excellent
accompaniment to cold meats.*

2 lbs cooking apples, peeled, cored and chopped	2 lb onions, finely chopped
1 lb Demerara sugar	1 pt malt vinegar
1 oz ground ginger	Pinch of mixed spice
	Salt to taste

Put all the ingredients into a preserving pan or a large heavy bottom saucepan. Bring to the boil and simmer for about $2^{1}/_{2}$ to 3 hours until the mixture thickens to the preferred consistency. Stir intermittently throughout the cooking period. Allow to cool, spoon into prepared jars and seal.

The Daily Portion

Porridge Oat Pastry

Porridge oats add a lovely texture to pastry.

4 oz flour   4 oz porridge oats   Pinch of salt
4 oz butter or margarine   1 egg, beaten

Set oven to 375°F or Mark 5. Grease an 8 inch flan tin. In a bowl, mix together the flour, oats and salt. Rub in the butter or margarine, then mix in the egg and knead with floured hands. Press the pastry into the flan tin, fill with baking beans and bake blind for 10 to 12 minutes. The pastry case is now ready for a filling as required. This pastry can also be used as a topping on meat and fish pies.

Vegetable Broth

A hearty soup filled with the flavours of root vegetables and barley. This recipe uses a turnip (not a swede) which in Scotland is known as a 'white turnip'.

1 oz butter	**1 large celery stick, chopped**
1 medium carrot, diced	**1¹/₂ pts vegetable or meat stock**
1 large onion, diced	**1 level tablespoon barley, well washed**
1 small white turnip, diced	**Salt and pepper**
1 leek, chopped	**Chopped fresh parsley or chives**

Melt the butter in a pan, add all the vegetables, cover with a lid and allow to sweat gently, shaking the pan to ensure they are well coated with butter. After about 5 to 6 minutes pour in the stock. Add the barley and bring to the boil. Season, reduce the heat and simmer gently for 1 to 1¹/₂ hours until the barley is soft. Serve with chopped fresh parsley or chives. Serves 4-6.

A Difficult Text

Mustard Lamb and Turnip Purry

A wonderfully tasty dish in which the flavours of the redcurrant, cream, wine and mustard complement the lamb.

| 3 lb leg of lamb | 2 teaspoons French mustard | Salt and pepper |
| 6 tablespoons red wine | 3 tablespoons redcurrant jelly | 3 fl oz soured cream |

THE PURRY
1 large turnip (swede)   Knob of butter   1 - 2 fl oz double cream
$^1/_2$ teaspoon ground cumin   Salt and pepper

Set oven to 350ºF or Mark 4. Rub the mustard over the lamb, season with a little salt and pepper and place in a roasting tin. Cook for approximately 1 hour 20 minutes, basting with the juices halfway through the cooking time. Set aside on a plate to rest. Pour off the fat from the tin, leaving the meat juices. Add the wine and redcurrant jelly to the tin, place on the heat and stir to mix all together. Stir in the cream and simmer until slightly thickened. Pour into a gravy boat. To make the purry, roughly chop the turnip and boil until soft. Drain and then mash with the butter, cream and cumin. Season to taste. To serve, slice the lamb thickly, pour over the sauce and add a helping of purry. Delicious with roast potatoes. Serves 4 to 6.

Claggum

2 teacups black treacle   1 teacup cold water

Put the treacle and water into a heavy pan and warm gently over a low heat. Then boil quickly until a little of the mixture, dropped into cold water, forms a soft ball between finger and thumb (238°F/114°C on a sugar thermometer). Pour into a greased, shallow tin. When cool enough to handle, pull out the toffee with hands lightly dusted with flour or icing sugar until it becomes pale and creamy in colour and twist into long sticks.

Roastit Bubbly-jock

Bubbly-jock is a Scottish name and probably derives from the gobbling sound of the turkey.

8-10 lb turkey   2 fl oz vegetable oil or melted butter   Turkey or chicken stock
1 tablespoon redcurrant jelly

STUFFINGS

<u>**Sausagemeat:**</u>   **2 oz fresh white breadcrumbs   8 oz sausagemeat   1 small onion, diced**
2 tablespoons chopped parsley   1 teaspoon chopped thyme   Salt & pepper   1 egg, beaten
<u>**Oyster:**</u> **4 oz fresh white breadcrumbs   ¼ pt milk   6 oysters (tinned/fresh)   Zest 1 lemon**
2 tablespoons chopped celery   Liver from turkey, chopped   1 tablespoon chopped parsley

First make the stuffings. For sausagemeat stuffing, mix all dry ingredients in a bowl and season. Bind with the egg and stuff mixture into crop end of the turkey. For oyster stuffing, first soak breadcrumbs in the milk. Add all other ingredients and season. Stuff tightly into the body of the bird and secure flap with a skewer. Set oven to 375ºF or Mark 5. Place stuffed turkey in a large roasting tin. Brush with oil or butter and cover with kitchen foil (also oiled or buttered). Roast for 20 to 25 minutes per lb. Baste about halfway through cooking time and remove foil about 20 minutes before the end. Place turkey on a serving dish and allow to rest. Drain fat from roasting tin, leaving the meat juices. Add sufficient stock (preferably made from turkey giblets but chicken stock will be satisfactory) and redcurrant jelly. Transfer tin to the heat to boil and reduce. Serve the sauce separately.

Savoury Potato Cakes

Excellent for breakfast or high tea and delicious topped with a poached egg.

2 rashers bacon, diced	Pepper to season
1 small leek or onion, finely chopped	1 egg, beaten
2 oz mushrooms, chopped	3 tablespoons fine oatmeal
8 oz cold mashed potatoes	Oil for frying

Put the bacon, leek or onion and mushrooms in a frying pan (no oil may be needed if the bacon used produces enough fat) and cook gently until the vegetables have softened. Set aside to cool. Mash the potato well in a bowl and add the bacon, leek or onion and mushrooms and season to taste. Mix well and shape into flat cakes about ¼ inch thick. Dip into the beaten egg, coat with oatmeal and fry in hot oil until lightly browned on both sides. Serve hot.

The New Toy

Honey Ice Cream

The natural sweetness of the honey makes a dreamy ice cream. Top with
Drambuie liqueur and pouring cream for a real Highland treat.

6 egg yolks   **¹/₄ pt clear honey**   **³/₄ pt double cream**
Drambuie liqueur, according to taste   ¹/₄ pt single cream

Beat the egg yolks in a bowl until light and fluffy. Heat the honey gently in a saucepan until it just reaches boiling point. Remove from the heat. Allow to cool slightly then pour the honey over the egg yolks, beating continuously. Next, beat in the double cream, return to the pan and gently heat the mixture to thicken it, taking care not to let it boil. Remove from the heat and transfer to a deep freezer container. Allow to cool, but keep whisking so that a skin does not form. Place in the freezer. After about two hours remove and whisk vigorously, to prevent ice crystals forming. Replace in the freezer until set firm. To serve, remove from the freezer about ten minutes before serving, place in individual dessert dishes and pour a little Drambuie and cream over the ice cream.

Caramel Shortbread

A delicious variation on plain shortbread for those who have a sweet tooth!

4 oz butter   4 oz caster sugar   5 oz self raising flour   Pinch of salt

TOPPING
4 oz butter   4 oz caster sugar
1 dessertspoon golden syrup   Small tin condensed milk

Set oven to 350ºF or Mark 4. Cream the butter and sugar together in a bowl, mix in the flour and salt and knead into a ball. Press into a greased shallow tin, about 11 x 7 inches and bake for about 20 minutes. Leave in the tin. For the topping, put all the ingredients into a saucepan and bring to the boil stirring continuously. Continue boiling until the mixture leaves the sides of the pan and starts to change colour. Then pour over the shortbread, spread out evenly and leave to cool. Cut into fingers when cold.

The Crofter's Grace

Cheese Soup and Dumplings

This hearty soup is a meal in itself.

1 oz butter   1 large onion, finely chopped   1 oz flour
1 level teaspoon dry mustard powder   ¹/₂ pt chicken or vegetable stock
³/₄ pt milk   Salt and pepper   4 oz Scottish cheddar cheese, grated

DUMPLINGS
2 oz porridge oats   1 oz shredded beef suet   1 small onion, finely chopped
1 tablespoon finely chopped fresh parsley or 1 dessertspoon dried parsley
1 egg, beaten well   Salt and pepper

In a large pan, melt the butter and cook the onion until soft. Stir in the flour and mustard powder and cook for 1 minute. Stir in the stock and milk, season and bring to the boil, stirring continuously. Cover and simmer for 15 minutes. Meanwhile, for the dumplings, put the oats, suet, onion, chopped or dried parsley and the seasoning into a bowl and bind with the beaten egg. Then divide and roll the mixture into small balls. Bring a saucepan of salted water to the boil and drop in the dumplings, simmering for about 15 minutes. Remove from the water and keep warm. Remove the soup from the heat when cooked, add the cheese and stir until melted. Add the dumplings and adjust the seasoning if necessary. Return to the heat and, when hot, serve immediately. Serves 4-6.

Ginger Flapjacks

So simple to make, flapjacks can be prepared in next to no time. If preferred, the ginger can be omitted.

6 oz butter   4 oz Demerara sugar   1 oz golden syrup
8 oz porridge oats   1 level teaspoon ground ginger

Set oven to 325°F or Mark 3. Put the butter, sugar and syrup together into a pan and heat gently until the sugar has melted. Remove from the heat and stir in the oats and ginger. Mix well. Press the mixture into a greased and base lined 8 inch sponge tin or similar and bake for 15 to 20 minutes. Allow to cool in the tin and mark into wedges or slices while still warm.

Rabbit Casserole

A real taste of the countryside. Either joint a whole fresh rabbit or use prepared joints if available.

6 - 8 rabbit joints	**1 tablespoon Demerara sugar**
Seasoned flour, to coat	**1 tablespoon French mustard**
2 oz butter	**1 pt chicken stock**
1 large onion, sliced	**A bayleaf**
2 streaky bacon rashers, diced	**Salt and pepper**
Chopped fresh parsley	

Set oven to 300ºF or Mark 2. Wash the rabbit joints in cold water, pat dry with kitchen paper and roll in the seasoned flour. Melt the butter in a flameproof casserole and brown the rabbit pieces. Add the onion and bacon and cook for 2 to 3 minutes. Dissolve the sugar and mustard in the stock and pour over the rabbit. Add the bayleaf and season with salt and pepper. Bring slowly to simmering point, cover and cook in the oven for $1\frac{1}{2}$ to 2 hours or until the meat is tender. Sprinkle with chopped parsley before serving. Serves 4.

Mince and Tatties

This variation on the plain mince and tatties recipe is full of extra vegetables;
children will never notice!

1 medium onion	2 teaspoons Bovril
1 medium carrot	1 teaspoon redcurrant jelly
2 oz turnip (swede)	1 teaspoon tomato purée
1 oz vegetable oil	1 tablespoon mushroom ketchup
1 lb best minced beef	1 stick of celery, left whole

Salt and pepper

Cut the onion, carrot and turnip (swede) into chunks and blitz in a food processor until finely chopped. Alternatively they can be well grated by hand. Heat the oil in a saucepan, add the mince and cook for 3 to 4 minutes. Add the finely chopped vegetables and cook for a further 2 to 3 minutes. Add all the other ingredients, including the stick of celery. Cover with water and bring to boiling point. Cover with a lid and simmer for 40 to 45 minutes. When cooked, remove the celery stick. Serve with buttery mashed potato. Serves 4.

Her Dochter's Bairn

Honey Cake

The honey makes this cake nice and moist.

3 oz butter	4 oz clear honey
3 oz sugar	8 oz self raising flour
2 eggs, beaten	1 level teaspoon baking powder

Set oven to 350°F or Mark 4. Grease and line a 7 inch round cake tin. Cream together the butter and sugar in a bowl. Add the eggs gradually and beat in the honey. Sift together the flour and baking powder and stir into the honey mixture. Transfer to the tin and bake for about 35 to 40 minutes or until a skewer inserted comes out clean. Leave in the tin for about 10 minutes to cool then turn out on to a wire rack.

Bread Patties

A very rich but tasty variation on vol-au-vents, with a chicken filling.
Not for calorie counters!

CASES
1 large loaf of stale white bread   **³/₄ pt single cream**   **1 - 2 eggs, beaten**
Toasted breadcrumbs   **Oil for frying**

FILLING
1 oz butter   **1 oz flour**   **¹/₄ pt chicken stock**   **Juice of ¹/₂ lemon**   **Salt and pepper**
12 oz cold cooked chicken, diced   **2 oz cooked ham, diced**   **4 oz mushrooms, chopped**

First make the filling. Melt the butter in a pan, stir in the flour and cook for 1 minute. Add the stock and lemon juice, season and stir over the heat until thickened. Add two tablespoons of the cream with the diced chicken, ham and mushrooms and heat through very thoroughly. Set aside and keep warm. For the bread cases, cut the bread into slices 2 inches thick and then cut out into 2 inch rounds with a pastry cutter. With a smaller cutter, cut the middle of each round halfway through and remove the bread from the centre (like a vol-au-vent case). Dip the rounds in the cream and drain well. Brush with beaten egg, coat with breadcrumbs and fry in hot oil until golden brown. Fill each case with the chicken mixture, reheat if necessary and serve hot. Makes about 18 patties.

The New Tack, or Lease

Stoved Chicken

'Stoved' dishes were so called because they were cooked on top of the range or stove rather than in the oven.

2 oz butter   4 small chicken breasts, skinned and sliced thinly
2 lb old potatoes, peeled and sliced about ¼ inch thick   Salt and pepper
2 large onions, sliced   1 pt chicken stock   2 tablespoons chopped parsley

Melt 1oz of the butter in a large heavy bottom saucepan or flameproof casserole and lightly brown the chicken slices. Remove from the pan and set aside. To assemble the dish in the pan or casserole, start with a thick layer of potatoes. Season, then add a layer of onion followed by a layer of chicken. Repeat until all have been used, ending with a layer of potatoes. Pour over the stock. Dot with small knobs of the remaining butter, bring to the boil, cover and simmer slowly for about 2 hours. Top up with a little water if it appears to be drying out too quickly. Sprinkle with parsley before serving. Serves 4.

Scots Tablet

Tablet has always been a Scottish favourite and is still a best seller at church fetes and bring-and-buy sales.

2 lb granulated sugar	**¼ pint milk**
4 oz butter	**Large tin condensed milk**
¼ pint water	**1 teaspoon vanilla essence**

Put the sugar, butter, water and milk into a large, heavy pan over a low heat and stir until the sugar has completely dissolved. Bring to the boil and boil for 10 minutes without stirring. Stir in the condensed milk and boil for a further 10 minutes. Remove from the heat and add the essence. Beat the mixture for 1 minute, then pour into a buttered, shallow tin and mark into squares. Cut when cold.

Apple and Bramble Crumble

Apples and blackberries always combine well together.

1 lb cooking apples, peeled, cored and sliced   8 oz blackberries
4 - 6 oz granulated sugar, to taste

CRUMBLE
4 oz flour   2 oz porridge oats   Pinch of salt
4 oz butter or margarine   4 oz Demerara sugar

Set oven to 375ºF or Mark 5. Mix together the apples and blackberries and put into a pie dish. Add the sugar according to taste and a little water. For the crumble, put the flour, oats, salt and butter or margarine into a bowl and work together with the hands until the mixture resembles breadcrumbs. Stir in the Demerara sugar and sprinkle the crumble mixture over the fruit. Bake for about 15 minutes and then reduce the temperature to 350ºF or Mark 4 and bake for a further 35 to 40 minutes or until the top is lightly browned.

Annie Hogg's Sweetbreads

This recipe is best made with lambs' sweetbreads, which have the most delicate flavour.

1 lb sweetbreads	**½ tin mushroom soup**
Seasoned flour, to coat	**8 fl oz milk**
1 oz butter	**2 tablespoons chopped parsley**
1 medium onion, finely chopped	**Salt and pepper**

Put the sweetbreads into a saucepan and cover with cold water. Bring to the boil, cover and simmer for 5 minutes. Drain, return to the saucepan and cover with fresh cold water. Leave until firm then remove from the water and trim off any stringy tissues. Set oven to 325°F or Mark 3. Toss the sweetbreads in seasoned flour and put into a greased casserole. To make the sauce, melt the butter in a pan, add the onion and gently cook until transparent. Add the mushroom soup, milk and chopped parsley. Stir and bring gently to the boil. Season and pour over the sweetbreads then cook for 1½ to 2 hours or until tender. Serve with mashed potato to mop up the lovely sauce. Serves 4.

The Light of the Home

Baked Apples with Walnut Butterscotch Sauce

Apples, whisky and butterscotch are very traditionally Scottish.

**6 large Bramley apples, cored   4 oz raisins   2 tablespoons whisky
2 tablespoons apple juice**

BUTTERSCOTCH SAUCE
**4 oz butter   2 tablespoons golden syrup   2 tablespoons black treacle
4 oz soft brown sugar   5 fl oz double cream   3 oz chopped walnuts**

Set oven to 350ºF or Mark 4. Put the raisins into a bowl with the whisky and leave to soak for 15 minutes. With a sharp knife score around the circumference of each apple to help to prevent it bursting during cooking. Place the apples in an oven-proof dish and stuff with the soaked raisins. Put into the oven and cook for about 35 to 40 minutes. Meanwhile make the sauce. Melt the butter, syrup and treacle in a heavy bottom pan. Add the sugar and stir continuously until it has dissolved and the mixture is bubbling. Remove from the heat and stir in the cream. Bring back to the boil, remove from the heat and stir in the chopped walnuts. Remove the apples from the oven, pour over the butterscotch sauce and serve immediately.

Roast Pheasant

The rich sauce complements the game flavour of the pheasant.

**1 pheasant, prepared   3 rashers bacon   2 oz butter, melted   5 fl oz white wine
1 tablespoon redcurrant jelly   Juice of ½ lemon   4 slices fried white bread**

STUFFING
**8 oz pork sausagemeat   1 small onion, finely chopped
1 dessert apple, peeled, cored and finely chopped   2 tablespoons chopped parsley
Salt and pepper   1 egg, beaten**

Set oven to 350ºF or Mark 4. First make the stuffing. In a bowl, mix together the sausagemeat, onion, apple, parsley and seasoning. Bind with the beaten egg. Stuff the pheasant (any stuffing left over can be shaped into balls and cooked round the bird). Place the pheasant in a roasting tin and wrap the bacon rashers round the bird. Brush all over with the butter and roast for about 35 to 40 minutes. Remove from the oven and drain off the fat. Pour the wine over the pheasant with the redcurrant jelly and lemon juice. Return to the oven for about another 20 to 25 minutes, basting frequently. Meanwhile, fry 4 slices of bread. When the pheasant is cooked and the juices run clear when a skewer is inserted, remove from the oven and cut into quarters. Place the pieces on the fried bread and keep warm. Transfer the roasting tin to the heat to boil and reduce the sauce. Pour over the pheasant to serve. For a brace of pheasants, double the ingredients but the cooking time remains the same.

An Auld Licht

Fife Bannocks

This plain bannock is, essentially, a large round scone. Traditionally it was cooked on a girdle, but baking in the oven is equally satisfactory. Also, buttermilk would have been used in this recipe.

6 oz flour	**Pinch of salt**
4 oz oatmeal	**1 teaspoon sugar**
¹/₂ teaspoon bicarbonate of soda	**1 oz butter**
³/₄ teaspoon cream of tartar	**About 6 - 8 tablespoons milk**

Set oven to 425°F or Mark 7. Put all the dry ingredients into a bowl and rub in the butter. Mix into a dough with just sufficient milk so that it leaves the sides of the bowl clean. Turn out on to a floured surface, knead lightly and press or roll out into a large round about ³/₄ inch thick. Cut into 4 quarters, put on to a greased baking sheet and bake in the oven for about 20 to 25 minutes until light golden brown. Alternatively, bake on a greased hot girdle. Serve sliced through with plenty of butter and raspberry jam.

Onion Gravy

This quick gravy is ideal for vegetarian dishes but is equally delicious served with cold or hot meats.

2 medium onions, finely sliced   2 oz butter   2 tablespoons flour
2 teaspoons Marmite   ³/₄ pt water

Melt the butter in a heavy bottom pan, add the onions and cover. Cook the onions slowly until soft and deep caramel brown, stirring from time to time. When browned, remove from the heat, add the flour, stir and return to the heat for 1 minute. Add the Marmite and water and stir until smooth. Continue to cook gently for a further 15 minutes, stirring occasionally.

Boiled Cake

Boiled cake is very quick and easy to prepare.

4 oz butter or margarine   ½ pt water
4 oz caster sugar   1 lb mixed dried fruit
Pinch of bicarbonate of soda   8 oz self raising flour
2 eggs, beaten

Set oven to 325°F or Mark 3. Grease and line an 8 inch round cake tin. In a saucepan, mix together the butter or margarine, sugar, bicarbonate of soda, water and dried fruit and bring to the boil. Boil for 2 minutes and then simmer for a further 15 minutes. Remove from the heat and allow to cool. Fold in the flour and eggs and transfer to the cake tin. Bake for 1½ to 2 hours or until a skewer inserted comes out clean. Leave in the tin for 10 minutes to cool then transfer to a wire rack.

Poacher's Soup

A lovely, rich country soup which uses the left-overs from any kind of game; pheasant, partridge, rabbit, hare etc. Also a white turnip, not a swede.

Carcasses of cooked game
Scraps of cooked game meat
1 tablespoon bacon fat or oil
2 medium carrots, roughly chopped
2 large onions, roughly chopped
1 white turnip, roughly chopped
1 stick celery, diced
1 bay leaf
Sprig of fresh thyme
8 peppercorns
3 pts vegetable stock
1-2 tablespoons sherry
2 fl oz double cream for serving

First, heat the fat in a large saucepan. Add the vegetables, cover and cook gently for 5 minutes taking care not to let them brown. Remove from the heat. Add the broken up carcasses, the herbs and peppercorns and the stock, reserving a little stock for blending. Bring to the boil, cover and simmer for 2 to 3 hours until the stock is really well flavoured. Strain and return to the saucepan. In a blender or food processor, purée the scraps of meat with a little of the stock until smooth. Return to the pan with any remaining stock. Season and bring to the boil so that the meat is well heated through. Stir in the sherry (amount according to preference) and serve with a swirl of double cream in each bowl. Serves 6.

Best Friends

Honeyed Oat Breakfast

A tasty and healthy way to start the day.

2 tablespoons clear honey   **$^1/_2$ pt milk or more if a thinner consistency preferred**
6 tablespoons porridge oats   2 tablespoons wheat or bran flakes
2 tablespoons chopped nuts   2 tablespoons raisins

Combine together the milk and honey, then add the liquid to all the other ingredients and mix thoroughly. This mixture is delicious topped with slices of fresh fruit. Make at least 30 minutes before serving. Serves 2.

Steak in Whisky Sauce

Best Scotch beef with whisky combine two of Scotland's finest products.

4 steaks, rump, sirloin or fillet	**1 oz mushrooms, finely chopped**
2 oz butter	**6 tablespoons whisky**
1 small onion, finely chopped	**2 teaspoons Worcestershire sauce**

Season the steaks with salt and pepper. Melt the butter in a frying pan. Fry the steaks until cooked to personal taste, turning midway through the cooking period. Set aside and keep warm. Fry the onion and mushrooms in the steak juices for about 3 to 4 minutes, then add the whisky and Worcestershire sauce. Return the steak to the pan and bring to the boil. Adjust the seasoning and re-heat the meat. Serve with new potatoes. Serves 4.

Granny's Comfort

Butterscotch Shortbread

A shortbread with a richer, darker colour than the usual recipe.

4 oz butter, softened	**5 oz flour**
2 oz soft dark brown sugar	**1 oz ground almonds**
5 drops vanilla essence	**Caster sugar for sprinkling**

Set oven to 300°F or Mark 2. Well grease a baking tray. In a bowl, cream the butter with 1oz of the sugar. Add the vanilla essence and continue creaming. Gradually work in the flour and the ground almonds. Mix in the remaining sugar. Turn out on to a floured surface and knead well. Press out or roll into a round about $^1/_2$ inch thick and place on the baking tray. Prick all over with a fork and sprinkle with caster sugar. Bake for 35 to 40 minutes until dark golden brown. Transfer to a wire rack to cool and cut into triangles.

Bruléed Raspberries with Whisky

Scottish wild raspberries are in season in July and August.

1 lb raspberries	**¹/₂ pt double cream**
1 tablespoon whisky	**1 teaspoon grated orange rind**
Caster sugar to taste	**3 oz soft light brown sugar**

Spread the raspberries over the base of a shallow, flameproof dish and sprinkle over the whisky and a little sugar to taste. Whip the double cream until thick and then fold in the orange rind. Spread evenly over the raspberries and chill in the refrigerator. When the pudding is required, preheat a hot grill. Cover the cream with about ¹/₂ inch thickness of brown sugar, place under the grill and cook until the sugar melts and bubbles. The pudding can either be served immediately or left to cool and harden.

Rich Venison Casserole

This casserole has a rich, game taste; a real flavour of the Highlands.

2 lb venison, cubed	5 fl oz port
2 tablespoons vegetable oil or dripping	8 oz cranberries
4 oz smoked bacon, diced	8 oz chestnuts
1 large onion, roughly diced	4 oz button mushrooms
1 oz flour	1 bayleaf
1½ pts beef stock	Salt and pepper

3 fl oz double cream

Set oven to 275°F or Mark 1. Heat the fat in a flameproof casserole and brown the venison cubes. Add the bacon and onion and cook for 3 to 4 minutes. Stir in the flour and cook for 1 minute, then pour in the stock and port and add the cranberries, chestnuts, mushrooms and bayleaf. Season to taste, bring slowly to simmering point, cover and cook in the oven for 2 to 2½ hours or until the meat is tender. Remove from the oven and stir in the cream. Serve with creamy mashed potato. Serves 4 to 6.

METRIC CONVERSIONS

The weights, measures and oven temperatures used in the preceding recipes can be easily converted to their metric equivalents. The conversions listed below are only approximate, having been rounded up or down as may be appropriate.

Weights

Avoirdupois	Metric
1 oz.	just under 30 grams
4 oz. (¼ lb.)	app. 115 grams
8 oz. (½ lb.)	app. 230 grams
1 lb.	454 grams

Liquid Measures

Imperial	Metric
1 tablespoon (liquid only)	20 millilitres
1 fl. oz.	app. 30 millilitres
1 gill (¼ pt.)	app. 145 millilitres
½ pt.	app. 285 millilitres
1 pt.	app. 570 millilitres
1 qt.	app. 1.140 litres

Oven Temperatures

	°Fahrenheit	Gas Mark	°Celsius
Slow	300	2	150
	325	3	170
Moderate	350	4	180
	375	5	190
	400	6	200
Hot	425	7	220
	450	8	230
	475	9	240

Flour as specified in these recipes refers to plain flour unless otherwise described.